What NOT to Do in Love!

What NOT to Do in Love!
Copyright © 2005 Sweetwater Press
Produced by Cliff Road Books

All rights reserved. No part of this book may be reproduced in any form or by any electronic or mechanical means, including information storage and retrieval systems, without written permission of the publisher.

Printed in The United States of America

ISBN: 1-58173-407-7

Cover design by Miles Parsons

This work is a compilation from numerous sources. Every effort has been made to ensure accuracy. However, the publisher cannot be responsible for incorrect information.

What NOT to Do in Love!

Compiled and Edited by
Linda J. Beam

SWEET WATER PRESS

About the Author

Linda J. Beam holds a B.A. in English from Judson College, and an M.A. in English from the University of Alabama at Birmingham. Her extensive editorial experience includes work with medical journals and textbooks, and a variety of corporate publications. In addition, she has developed and presented business communication seminars on business writing, and basic grammar and punctuation. She currently works as Managing Editor at Crane Hill Publishers in Birmingham, Alabama.

Other works by Linda include *What NOT to Say!, What NOT to Name Your Baby!, What NOT to Do in Polite Company!, What NOT to Do at Work!,* and *What's Your Bible I.Q.?*

Contents

"How Do I Love Thee?" 7

"Looking for Love (in All the Wrong Places)": Finding Mr. / Ms. Right ... 9

"Smooth Operator": Flirting.. 23

"Like to Get to Know You": Asking for a Date 29

"Could It Be Magic": First Dates.. 35

"Put Your Head on My Shoulder": Dating Etiquette 45

"Ain't No Mountain High Enough": Meeting Your Date's Parents 51

"Are You Lonesome Tonight": Dating as a Single Parent...................... 57

"To Know You Is to Love You": Office Romances 63

"I Just Called to Say I Love You": Long Distance Relationships.......... 69

"You Don't Bring Me Flowers": Giving Gifts to Your Loved One 75

"Have I Told You Lately that I Love You?": Writing a Love Letter 81

"I'm Sorry": Resolving Conflict 87

"Your Cheatin' Heart": Handling an Unfaithful Lover 93

"Bye Bye Love": Breaking Up.. 97

"With This Ring": Buying an Engagement Ring.................................. 105

"Hopelessly Devoted to You": Proposing 111

"Get Me to the Church on Time": Planning a Wedding 117

"There's a Place for Us": Arranging Your Honeymoon....................... 127

"Love and Marriage": Enjoying Life as Newlyweds............................ 133

"Forever and Ever, Amen": Having a Happy Marriage 139

"How Do I Love Thee?"

With these simple words, Elizabeth Barrett Browning began what has become one of the most famous love poems of all times. Her eloquent phrases speak of love given freely, purely, quietly, even eternally.

Heady stuff. For most of us, though, love is more practical. It's made up of stages and details that have to be handled with care. You have to meet the right person, stay with the relationship long enough to get to know each other, maintain and nurture the relationship as it grows, maybe even through breaking up and making up, and finally, see that any commitment you make meets the expectations of both parties involved.

With all the variables in a successful love relationship, it's almost a miracle that people meet, marry, and stay that way. Lots of things have to work out just right. *What NOT to Do in Love!* offers guidelines to help make that possible. And for the times when relationships end, it offers commonsense directions to help get past the loss.

No matter what your relationship scenario, *What NOT to Do in Love!* has pointers that can help. When you consider what's at stake, it couldn't hurt!

"Looking for Love (in All the Wrong Places)": Finding Mr. / Ms. Right

"Looking for Love (in All the Wrong Places)": Finding Mr. / Ms. Right

Be proactive in looking for the right person. There are general things you can do to meet someone interesting and particular things as well. Both are listed below.

What NOT to Do

- Do not wait for others to take the initiative.

- Do not settle for dating someone that you have no interest in just for the sake of having someone to date. You'll be wasting precious time that could be spent with someone who is perfect for you.

- Draft a personal ad even if you do not intend to send it. The exercise will force you to be specific about what kind of person you hope to find.

- Do not date a co-worker without knowing your company's policy on it, or if policy prohibits it.

- Do not overlook public places such as the library or grocery store for meeting a potential date.

> "We come to love not by finding the perfect person, but by learning to see an imperfect person perfectly."
> Sam Keen

- Do not ask for anyone's phone number if you are not really interested in contacting them.

- Do not give anyone else your phone number if you are not interested in hearing from them. If they call, you'll have to think of a way to avoid them.

- Do not rely on false confidence to help you meet people, like the high induced by drugs or alcohol.

"Looking for Love (in All the Wrong Places)": Finding Mr. / Ms. Right

- Do not think only of external appearances. Think about what people are like on the inside.

What to Do

- Make sure you have dealt with ghosts from previous relationships, and that you are ready to try again.

- Decide who you are and the kind of person that would interest you.

- Develop a plan for getting out of the house and into places where potential dates might be.

- Become involved in activities where you have a genuine interest, not just where you think a possible date might be.

- Move slowly when you meet someone new. Just because he/she is available does not mean they are the perfect match for you.

- Cultivate a wide circle of friends. The more people you know, the greater your chances of finding the right person to date.

- Look around at your everyday activities. There may be people you are overlooking. Familiar places like church and school offer opportunities to meet people with your same interests.

- Become a "regular" at some place like a coffeehouse where you can meet people.

The release of Will Smith's film <u>Hitch</u> focused attention on dating coaches, a new approach to dating. Coaches offer advice and strategy to help you get through common dating dilemmas, and tips on specific problems like overcoming shyness and getting over a broken heart.

"Looking for Love (in All the Wrong Places)": Finding Mr. / Ms. Right

- Be open to consider dating people who might not exactly fit your ideal for a date. You might be surprised to find someone with attractive qualities that you had not considered.

- Be yourself.

- Consider sending an anonymous note to let someone know of your interest in him or her.

- Ask someone you trust to tell the other person about your interest in him or her.

ONLINE

Online dating services use modern technology to match likes and dislikes between people looking for dates. It is an objective way to identify people with whom you share common interests.

What NOT to Do

- Do not create a persona you cannot live up to. Lies will eventually catch up to you, so be honest in representing yourself.

- Do not get overly excited when you learn that your name and particulars have been matched with others. These are only possibilities, not matches. It will take time and effort, and only you and the other person can determine if a true match has been made.

- Do not take at face value everything that another person tells you. Be cautious until you are sure that everything you have been told is true.

- Do not idealize anyone you meet online. Hours of chatting cannot take the place of meeting and getting to know the other person.

"Looking for Love (in All the Wrong Places)": Finding Mr. / Ms. Right

- Do not treat a date with someone you met online the same as you would a date set up by a friend. Remember that the people you meet online are strangers.

- Do not meet the person you got to know online without letting someone else know where you will be and with whom.

- Do not use terminology or abbreviations that readers will not recognize.

- Do not give out your home address to the person until you get to know him or her.

- Do not send too many e-mail messages when a contact is made, or you will appear to be needy.

> **A recent survey shows that the top three reasons people respond to an online ad are because they liked the picture, they liked the description of the person, and they liked their interests.**

- Do not respond to anyone's ad a second time if he or she did not acknowledge your initial response.

- Do not become involved with so many people from ads that you are not able to give adequate attention to any of them.

- Do not talk about personal details, particularly about anything intimate, during your first conversations.

- Do not put too much pressure on yourself to meet someone from an online search.

"Looking for Love (in All the Wrong Places)": Finding Mr. / Ms. Right

What to Do

- Check out several online services before signing up with one. Find one that fits your goals.

- Choose an online dating service that will allow you to retain your privacy until you are ready to reveal personal details to prospective dates.

- Pick a "name" that truly describes you. Silly names may be entertaining, but it is much better to use something that tells something about you, such as "Dog-lover."

- Provide a valid e-mail address so that those interested in meeting you can contact you.

- Write your ad carefully. Be honest, specific, and brief.

- Use simple language for your ad.

- Check your grammar and spelling.

> **The first online dating service was WebPersonals.com, started in 1993.**

- If pictures may be included, use a current one.

- Indicate specifically what you are looking for in another person.

- Be honest about your current status, whether you are married, separated, or single.

- Visit chat rooms that attract people you would want to get to know. Observe a while before you begin to participate.

- Remember that you may want to meet the people you "chat" with one day, and act accordingly. If and when you meet someone in person that you've already met online, you do not want your first words to be an apology for a careless online comment.

"Looking for Love (in All the Wrong Places)": Finding Mr. / Ms. Right

- Proceed slowly with a new relationship.

- Be patient in expecting replies to your ad. Other people may be as careful in considering their response as you were in writing your ad.

- Include information about some characteristic or interest that is uniquely yours.

- Be positive and courteous in all of your dealings with others, even if you mutually decide not to pursue a relationship.

> One online dating service reports that when it started ten years ago, it signed up sixty thousand people in its first year. Now it signs up that many daily.

PERSONAL ADS

Personal ads are a great way to meet people that you might not normally come in contact with. The following suggestions will help you write an ad that will get results!

What NOT to Do

- Do not lie about personal details to impress someone.

- Do not write your life story, but provide enough details to give an idea of your interests.

- Do not use cliché words and phrases in describing yourself.

- Do not focus too heavily on any one thing when describing yourself. You will appear to be one-dimensional.

- Do not offer your home phone number in the ad. Use your cell number or e-mail address instead. You may want to set up a special e-mail account just for responses to your ad.

"Looking for Love (in All the Wrong Places)": Finding Mr. / Ms. Right

- Do not offer other identifying details that would allow anyone to track you down before you are ready.
- Do not believe everything you read about another person. The process of getting to know each other will take time.
- Do not communicate with so many people from the ads at one time that you cannot give each adequate consideration.
- Do not feel pressured to meet people before you are ready.

What to Do
- Consider placing your ad in a paper that appeals to particular interests you have, such as a sports paper, or a magazine for your favorite hobby.
- Gather information about requirements for your ad.
- Give careful thought to what your ad will say.
- Be specific about the kinds of things that interest you, and the kind of person you hope to meet.
- Use a current picture if you include one.
- State your current relationship status honestly.
- Place your ad in a local paper so you will be assured of dating someone that lives nearby.

The original personal ad? Mail order brides were popular with early settlers in America, the majority of which were men, who wrote to Europe to find a wife because they could not find one locally. The concept has been revived and has flourished in recent days, thanks to the Internet.

"Looking for Love (in All the Wrong Places)": Finding Mr. / Ms. Right

- List your assets, but do not brag.
- Be specific about what type of relationship you are searching for. Do you just want a companion, or is romance the goal?
- Tell what is unique about you. Highlight interesting information about yourself such as an unusual hobby or vocation.
- Use proper grammar and spelling in your ad.
- Use recognizable abbreviations in preparing your ad. Those commonly used include, but are not limited to, the following:

    A - Asian
    B - Black
    BBW - Big Beautiful Woman
    BHM - Big Handsome Man
    BiF - Bi Sexual Female
    BiM - Bi Sexual Male
    C - Christian
    D - Divorced
    DDF - Drug/Disease Free
    F - Female
    FTA - Fun Travel Adventure
    G - Gay
    GSOH - Good Sense of Humor
    H - Hispanic
    HWP - Height Weight Proportional
    IRL - In Real Life
    ISO - In Search Of
    J - Jewish
    LD - Light Drinker

"Looking for Love (in All the Wrong Places)": Finding Mr. / Ms. Right

LDS - Latter Day Saints
LS - Light Smoker
LTR - Long Term Relationship
M - Male
MM - Marriage Minded
NA - Native American
NBM - Never Been Married
ND - Non Drinker
NS - Non Smoker
P - Professional
S - Single
SD - Social Drinker
SI - Similar Interests
SOH - Sense of Humor
TS - Transsexual
W - White
W/ - With
W/O - Without
YO - Years Old

- Keep track of results to see which ads are the most effective.

"Looking for Love (in All the Wrong Places)": Finding Mr. / Ms. Right

SPEED DATING

Speed dating utilizes a round-robin format to help daters meet several people one-on-one at the same event. Interested people meet at a given location, then rotate through brief meetings with possible dates. Each "date" typically lasts ten minutes or less before you move onto the next potential mate. Here are some guidelines for this unique way to meet your special someone.

What NOT to Do

- Do not dress too casually for speed dating, even if the sponsor of the event says dress is casual. Dress as you would for a first date.

- Do not use cliché first lines.

> Speed dating was begun in 1999 by Rabbi Raacov Deyo and is based on the Jewish tradition of chaperoned gatherings of Jewish young people. It was originally intended as a way to encourage Jewish young people to marry within their faith, but the concept has spread to the secular community as well.

- Do not exchange contact information with the people you meet. At the end of the evening, each dater will submit a list of people they would like to see again, and event organizers will provide contact information as needed.

- Do not lie about yourself. You want people to be attracted to you based on who you really are, not who you pretend to be.

"Looking for Love (in All the Wrong Places)": Finding Mr. / Ms. Right

- Do not give out personal details about yourself. That can come later with the people you decide to date.

- Do not give mixed signals. Do not lead the other person to think you will deliver more than you honestly intend to.

- Do not pressure others to request a match with you.

- Do not try to dominate the conversation. Give the other person a chance to tell you about him or herself.

- Do not use offensive language during your meetings.

- Do not be discouraged if you don't find a match right away.

- Do not take rejection personally if someone you wanted to get to know does not feel the same.

What to Do

- Focus on topics appropriate for a first date, such as your job or current events.

> How do you know when you "click"? Some people say when "synchrony" occurs, that is, when two people meet, like each other, and begin to mirror each others' movements.

- Pay attention to details of your appearance. You will only have a very short time to make a good first impression.

- Concentrate on the conversation you have with the other person during the brief time allowed.

- Pay attention to your body language during each meeting so that you do not send out unintended negative signals. For example, crossed arms could make you seem defensive.

"Looking for Love (in All the Wrong Places)": Finding Mr. / Ms. Right

- Respect the other person by keeping your hands to yourself.
- Be yourself.
- Show interest in the other person by asking about his or her interests.

"Smooth Operator": Flirting

"Smooth Operator": Flirting

Flirting can help you get the attention of someone who interests you, let him or her know of your interest, and gauge if the interest is mutual.

What NOT to Do

- Do not worry so much about what others are thinking of you that you do not have a good time. If you are enjoying yourself, you will seem more interesting.

- Do not exhibit negative body language, such as crossing your arms defensively or looking distracted.

- Do not use offensive or sexually explicit language in your remarks.

- Do not invade the other person's personal space. If you receive a welcoming response, move a little closer, but be careful not to get so close as to make the other person uncomfortable.

> "There are times not to flirt: When you're sick. When you're with children. When you're on the witness stand."
> Joyce Jillson

- Do not fidget.

- Do not set up physical barriers, such as chairs, between yourself and the object of your flirting.

- Do not bunch together in groups with your friends: it would be intimidating to those you are flirting with.

- Do not encourage attention from anyone that truly does not interest you just to make yourself feel better.

"Smooth Operator": Flirting

> **Clues that the other person is interested vary by gender. Signs that a woman is interested include looking downward, touching her neck or hair, and tilting her head. Signs that a man is interested include moving his body to face you directly, adjusting his tie, and leaning toward you.**

- Do not look frozen or stiff. Be mobile in your expressions and movements.

- Do not give up if your interest is not returned. You may not get immediate results, but keep trying.

- Do not allow yourself to be maneuvered into being totally alone with someone you are flirting with. Until you know the person better, safety should be a major consideration.

What to Do

- Find the right place and time to flirt. At a bar, people are relaxed and open to conversation. But in the gym, people may be focused on getting through their workout.

- Get yourself in the right frame of mind. Don't think about the obstacles; think of the exciting new people you might get to know.

- Start by checking your self-esteem. The underlying key to all flirtation is confidence.

- Give yourself a pep talk about being an interesting person to get to know.

- Look approachable by smiling and looking at others.

"Smooth Operator": Flirting

- Break the ice by complimenting the other person on his or her clothes, or on some other feature that you find attractive.

- Make sure compliments are general and sincere.

- Be aware of what your body language is saying. You do not want to promise more than you are willing to do.

> **Clever, rehearsed opening lines seldom work because they seem insincere. Simple, natural remarks work best.**

- Ask open-ended questions to help initiate conversation. Recent movies or current events are safe topics that almost anyone will know about.

- Make direct eye contact with the other person when you flirt, but look away occasionally. An intense gaze may frighten the other person.

- Gauge the other person's interest and react accordingly. If you sense no positive response to your efforts, exit gracefully.

- Be careful that your flirting is not misunderstood. You do not want your actions to be mistaken for a sexual advance.

> **When you flirt, your body language is more important than your spoken language. A recent study found that when people form their initial impression of you, 55 percent is based on your appearance and body language, 38 percent on your style of speaking, and only 7 percent on what you actually say.**

"Smooth Operator": Flirting

- Watch the other person's body language. A scowl or other negative gestures will let you know your attention is not welcomed.
- Remember that flirting isn't about you; it's about showing the other person that you are attracted to him or her.
- Use humor in flirting, but don't tell an endless string of corny jokes.
- Be gracious if you are approached but are not interested.
- Move away from the group if someone approaches you that you would like to get to know better.

> **"Flirting is the gentle art of making a man feel pleased with himself."**
> Helen Rowland

"Like to Get to Know You": Asking for a Date

"Like to Get to Know You": Asking for a Date

You'll never know whether another person would like to go out with you until you ask! And that's simple if you follow the guidelines below.

What NOT to Do

- Do not wait for the other person to ask you. If you're interested, go ahead and take a chance.

- Do not expect anyone else to ask another person for you. Involving a third party is not a good idea.

- Do not ask anyone for a date just for the sake of going out with someone.

- Do not wait until the last minute to ask for a date.

- Do not just blurt out the invitation; ease into it.

Sadie Hawkins Day, which offers women the chance to ask men out on a date, made its debut in Al Capp's "Li'l Abner" comic strip on November 15, 1937. Sadie was "the homeliest gal in the hills" who got tired of waiting for men to court her. Worried that she would never leave home, her father, Hekzebiah, suggested a foot race in which unmarried gals pursued the town's bachelors. The prize for lucky women who caught their men was matrimony. Capp received so many letters in response that it became an annual event in the strip each November for four decades, and spawned similar events all over the United States.

"Like to Get to Know You": Asking for a Date

- Do not call and hang up. Most people have caller I.D. now, and you'll look foolish.

- Do not leave an invitation for a date on an answering machine. If the person you are calling to ask out is not home, you may leave your name and number for him or her to call you, or leave a brief message stating that you will call again.

- Do not be devastated if you are rejected. Assume the attitude that the other person has just missed out on an opportunity to get to know someone as interesting as you.

- Do not ask for a date at an inappropriate time, or in inappropriate surroundings. For instance, if you meet someone at a funeral, or during a time of crisis, wait until a better time to ask.

- Do not feel obliged to go out with anyone just because they ask. Gently, but firmly, decline if you are not interested.

- Do not compromise your integrity by suggesting or agreeing to any activity that you do not feel comfortable with on a date.

What to Do

- Introduce yourself if your intended date is someone you know only slightly, or someone you've heard about from a mutual friend.

- Indicate how you may already know each other. For example, "I'm a friend of John's, and we met at his graduation."

- Ask for a home phone number or address only if you are willing to share your own.

- Consider asking for the date on the telephone. If things don't go well, you can excuse yourself easily.

"Like to Get to Know You": Asking for a Date

> **Lovebirds, colorful birds found in Africa, are so named because they sit closely together in pairs, like lovers. Because they mate for life, they are symbols of loyalty and love.**

- Call at a time that will not be intrusive. If you e-mail, the other person can answer at his or her convenience, but this way is less personal.

- Ask for a date at a reasonable time in the future; a week to ten days in advance is average for a new relationship.

- Suggest meeting casually for the first time, say, for a cup of coffee. Then you can both decide if you would like to get together again.

- Offer to double date if you think the other person might be reluctant to go out alone.

- Have a general idea of what activity you'd like to suggest for your first date.

> **"Love is the master key that opens the gates of happiness."**
> Oliver Wendell Holmes

- Be specific when asking. Instead of just asking if the other person would like to go out sometime, state an activity that you are interested in, suggest a date, and then ask if he or she would like to accompany you.

- Offer options about your date so the other person can help tailor time together that you will both enjoy.

"Like to Get to Know You": Asking for a Date

- If you are refused, ask if another time would be better, or if the other person is simply not interested.
- Have a plan for a graceful exit just in case you are refused.

"Could It Be Magic":
First Dates

"Could It Be Magic": First Dates

First dates are a combination of excitement and dread, but you can have a good time by following a few commonsense suggestions.

What NOT to Do

- Do not plan an activity that you do not enjoy just because you think the other person likes it. Your first date will be stressful enough without trying to endure something you hate.

- Do not wear clothes that have slogans, especially negative ones.

- Do not wear clothes that make you feel stiff or uneasy.

- Do not wear suggestive or revealing clothing.

- Do not overdo fragrances. Besides the fact that they may be overpowering, your date may be allergic to them.

- Do not keep your date waiting. Be ready at the time you agreed upon.

- Do not expect your date to read your mind. If you are asked for your preference on plans for the evening, express your thoughts and feelings.

Love at first smell? Some scientists think that we fall in love not from the first sight of another, but from the first smell. Although we consciously pay attention to what we see and hear of the other person, subconsciously, the way he or she smells plays a big part in our reaction to the initial meeting.

"Could It Be Magic": First Dates

- Do not tell people how great you are—show them. Let your actions and conversation speak for itself.

- Do not be negative or complain about anything, even if things don't go as planned.

- Do not talk about former relationships or dark secrets. There will be time for that if the relationship progresses.

- Do not lie about your marital status, or anything else. If you continue to date, you will have to admit the truth eventually.

- Do not ask personal questions. Your date will offer details when and if they are appropriate.

- Do not agree with your date for the sake of agreeing. Politely express your opinion if it is different from his or hers.

- Do not complain if you are tired or don't feel well. If you truly aren't up to the date, postpone it until another time.

- Do not go into the details of your financial affairs.

- Do not plan an activity that is competitive. You do not want to feel that either of you has to best the other.

- Do not make unwanted sexual advances.

- Do not expect or offer intimacy as repayment for date expenses.

- Do not talk on your cell phone during your date. Your companion deserves your full attention.

- Do not interrupt your date while he or she is speaking.

- Do not use inappropriate or explicit language during your conversation.

"Could It Be Magic": First Dates

Candy has always said, "I'm sweet on you," but in 1860, Daniel Chase of the New England Confectionary Company invented the process to print messages directly onto candies. Originally, the candy was shaped like horseshoes and baseballs, but as time went on, the sayings became shorter, and the now-familiar heart shape was produced, which we know as conversation hearts. New sayings are continually added to keep the product current. The company estimates that about eight billion of the tiny messengers are sold between January 1 and February 14 each year.

- Do not order food that will be messy or embarrassing to eat.

- Do not use coupons for dinner or entertainment. Save them for another time.

- Do not order the most expensive thing on the menu unless you are paying.

- Do not rush the date. Take time to enjoy being together and getting to know each other.

- Do not be evasive about questions your date asks. Answer inquiries honestly and openly. If you truly don't want to answer a question, just say that you don't feel comfortable answering it.

- Do not respond to questions during conversation with a simple "Yes" or "No." Provide details that will give the other person a chance to know you.

"Could It Be Magic": First Dates

- Do not talk non-stop about yourself.
- Do not expect perfection.
- Do not take children with you.
- Do not suggest a first date on a date when there will be extra pressure, such as Valentine's Day, or New Year's Eve.
- Do not offer to help pay unless you can and are willing to do so.
- Do not continue to talk about subjects that you sense do not interest your date.
- Do not bring up controversial topics like religion or politics. There are plenty of neutral topics that can help you get to know each other.
- Do not smoke without asking if your date minds, and then, only in designated areas.
- Do not tolerate abusive or disrespectful behavior toward you.
- Do not hesitate to apologize if you accidentally offend your date.
- Do not try to impress your date by spending a lot of money. You'll look even worse when you scale back if you continue to date.

You're never too old for love! Minnie Munro became the world's oldest bride when she married Dudley Reid at the age of 102 on May 31, 1991. Her groom was a young whipper-snapper of 83. The oldest groom on record is 103-year-old Harry Stevens, who married spry 84-year-old Thelma Lucas on December 3, 1984.

"Could It Be Magic": First Dates

- Do not pretend to be interested in going on another date if you are not.

- Do not blame yourself if the date does not go well. You are not obligated to continue to see anyone that truly does not interest you.

What to Do

- Make plans to do something you both enjoy.

- Plan to do something that will allow you the opportunity to get to know each other. Going to a movie may be a classic way to spend an evening, but it does not allow for conversation.

- Get directions to your meeting place ahead of time so that you do not have to search for the location at the last minute.

- Pick a meeting place that is easy to find. There are enough stresses on a first date without adding the problem of meeting somewhere that's hard to find.

- Be considerate of the other person's schedule when making plans.

- Meet at a neutral place so you are both free to leave when you are ready.

- Talk with your date ahead of time to make sure what appropriate dress will be for your date.

- Invest time in looking your best. Pay careful attention to grooming, since your appearance will make an important statement before you ever say a word.

- Pay attention to personal hygiene. Take a bath and use deodorant before your date.

"Could It Be Magic": First Dates

- Dress attractively, but comfortably. Also, dress appropriately for the activity you plan.

- Compliment your date on how he or she looks.

- Keep your first date simple to minimize the pressure. You can "go all out" later.

- Meet for coffee or lunch if you are apprehensive about a date. It's easier to get through a quick meal like this than to drag through an entire dinner.

- Tell someone else where you are going and with whom.

- Be respectful of the other person's "personal space." Do not lean in or crowd the other person, and make him or her feel uncomfortable.

Some people believe that a girl is able to tell what sort of man she will marry by the first bird she sees on St. Valentine's Day. Common birds and the spouses they predict are:

Type of bird	Prediction
Blackbird	Priest
Blue bird	A happy man
Dove	A loving man
Robin	Sailor
Sparrow	Farmer
Woodpecker	Will not marry
Yellow bird	A rich man

"Could It Be Magic": First Dates

- Be cautious about drinking. It will lower your inhibitions, and you may display behavior you will regret.

- Look your date in the eyes as you talk and get to know each other.

- Use your best manners. Do not burp or scratch private parts of your body.

- Be courteous to people who help you, like your server at dinner, or the cashier at the theater. Your date will notice how you treat others.

> The Claddagh is an Irish love symbol that depicts two hands holding a heart that is wearing a crown. Friendship is represented by the two hands, while love is represented by the heart. The crown represents loyalty.

- Keep safety in mind when you meet, especially if your date is with someone you do not know well. Meet in a neutral place where you are not alone until you know each other better.

- Be flexible. If something goes wrong, adjust your plans without being upset. Attitude will be more important than what you actually do together.

- Take extra money just in case the unexpected happens.

- Ask open-ended questions to help you get to know the other person. Good topics to start with are his or her job, hometown, or hobbies.

- Listen to what your date says.

- Pace yourself. You don't have to know everything about your date in the first five minutes, and vice versa.

"Could It Be Magic": First Dates

- Pay attention to your date. Do not be distracted by other people or things around you.
- Stay positive even if your dates don't always go well.
- Remember to thank the other person for the date. Good manners make, and leave, a good impression.
- Plan to end the date early. If things don't work out, you will both be glad to end it. If things are going well when the set time comes, you can always stay later than planned.
- Follow up by calling or text-messaging to let your date know you had a good time and arrived home safely.
- Listen to your "gut feeling" about whether your date is a "keeper."
- Relax! It's only one date, and it can be over any time you choose.

> "I have learned not to worry about love, but to honor its coming with all my heart."
> Alice Walker

"Put Your Head on My Shoulder": Dating Etiquette

"Put Your Head on My Shoulder": Dating Etiquette

Dating is a time to get to know each other. Even in long-term relationships that become very comfortable and casual, your partner deserves to be treated with respect and courtesy. Here are some things to remember as your relationship develops.

What NOT To Do

- Do not call anyone you are dating several times a day. You will appear to be desperate.

- Do not date anyone who is married. Even if he or she is willing to continue to date, the existing relationship should be ended before pursuing a new one.

- Do not buy expensive or personal presents for someone you are dating unless the relationship is serious.

- Do not promise to call unless you really intend to do so.

- Do not mislead about your intentions. If you are looking for a serious relationship, or if your dating is only casual, make sure to be honest.

The world's longest kiss occurred in London in July of 2005 when James Belshaw and his girlfriend, Sophia Severin, shared an unbroken kiss for 31 hours, 30 minutes, and 30 seconds. Throughout the event, they were not allowed to sit, or fall asleep; they could only take nourishment through a straw; and they had to continue kissing even while going to the restroom.

"Put Your Head on My Shoulder": Dating Etiquette

- Do not make a habit of breaking dates. Do so only on rare occasions and only with good reason.

- Do not cancel plans with little or no notice. If you must change plans, try to give advance notice.

- Do not keep your date waiting. Be ready at the time agreed upon.

- Do not betray confidences that your partner has shared with you.

- Do not habitually make your plans at the last minute. Doing so will leave the impression that you only plan dates when you lack something else to do.

- Do not cancel a date to accept a date with someone else.

- Do not reveal personal details of the relationship to other people. Keep those between yourself and your partner.

- Do not complain if you are tired or don't feel well. If you aren't up to the date, reschedule it.

- Do not try to force your opinions or preferences on the other person. Allow him or her to help decide how your time together should be spent.

- Do not continue to pursue someone who is obviously not interested in dating you.

- Do not try to make him or her jealous by flirting with someone else.

What to Do
- Settle grievances with previous lovers so that you do not bring old issues into a new relationship.

- Be willing to pay for the date if you are the one who asked for it.

"Put Your Head on My Shoulder": Dating Etiquette

- Always be on time. Call if you will be late.
- Be interested in what your date has to say.
- Smile and make eye contact while communicating with your date.
- Compliment your date on his or her appearance. People always like to know that their efforts to look nice are noticed.
- Respect your partner's privacy. No matter how long you have been dating, do not open his or her mail, look at financial information, etc., without his or her permission.

> **To celebrate one hundred years of filmmaking, the American Film Institute identified America's one hundred greatest love stories. Number one on the list was Casablanca. Other top-ten favorites included West Side Story, Roman Holiday, An Affair to Remember, The Way We Were, and, of course, Love Story.**

- Plan your dates ahead of time instead of getting into a cycle of "I don't know what to do."
- Display good manners in every aspect of your relationship.
- Consult your date before you make plans that include other people. He or she may prefer not to socialize with some of the people you plan to include.
- Consider your schedules when planning activities. End your time together early when either of you has important plans for the next day.

"Put Your Head on My Shoulder": Dating Etiquette

- Learn from mistakes in past relationships and try not to repeat them.

- Listen when your partner tries to communicate with you.

- Focus on your date when you are together. Do not pay more attention to other people than to your date, and do not spend time on your cell phone while you are together.

- Make sure you both understand the nature of your relationship, such as if you will date each other exclusively, or whether you are free to continue to date others.

- Talk with your partner if there is something about your relationship that concerns you. Do not wait for him or her to ask what's wrong.

- Be loyal to the person you are dating. Do not talk in a negative way about him or her to other people.

- Express appreciation for the things your partner does for you, whether it is opening the door for you, or making arrangements for a special date.

- Keep promises that you make to your partner.

- Honor your partner by speaking well of him or her to other people.

- Examine and talk honestly about differences and similarities that may prevent or promote a long-term relationship.

> "The one thing we can never get enough of is love. And the one thing we never give enough is love."
> Henry Miller

"Ain't No Mountain High Enough": Meeting Your Date's Parents

"Ain't No Mountain High Enough": Meeting Your Date's Parents

Meeting your date's parents is a special occasion. Whether you and your date's relationship is casual or serious, you will want to make a good impression by observing a few commonsense rules.

What NOT to Do

- Do not be late.

- Do not wear inappropriate or offensive clothing.

- Do not wear heavy fragrance. The people you are meeting may be allergic to it.

- Do not use their first names unless they ask you to.

- Do not use profanity or offensive language.

- Do not argue with them.

- Do not brag to impress them.

- Do not lie about anything.

- Do not disrespect your date (their family member) in their presence. Make a special effort to see that nothing goes wrong.

- Do not get defensive about questions that the parent(s) may ask you. They are only asking because they are naturally interested in anything that affects their family member.

> Cupid, the most famous of Valentine symbols, has always played a role in the celebrations of love and lovers. With arrows from his bow, he shoots gods and humans, causing them to fall deeply in love.

"Ain't No Mountain High Enough": Meeting Your Date's Parents

- Do not be overly affectionate with your date in front of his or her parents.

- Do not bring up controversial topics like politics. Stay with more neutral subjects.

- Do not bring up other topics that you have learned will be sensitive.

- Do not show disrespect for their opinions and thoughts, even if you do not share them. Your date will be watching to see how you deal with his or her parents, as well as to see what they think of you.

- Do not smoke.

- Do not drink too much. You cannot predict the effect it will have on your behavior.

- Do not make a scene about anything that happens. For example, if you are dining out together, react calmly to food or service mishaps.

- Do not tell off-color jokes or use humor that might be misunderstood.

- Do not worry if the first meeting does not go well.

What to Do

- Learn about the family ahead of time so you will know what to expect.

- Find out if there are sensitive subjects that should not be brought up.

- Relax and be yourself.

- Dress nicely. Do not wear skimpy or revealing clothing that will embarrass you or others.

"Ain't No Mountain High Enough": Meeting Your Date's Parents

- Use your best manners. Offer to help with dishes; say "Please" and "Thank you."

- Look the parents in the eye. If you avoid looking directly at them, you may appear to be hiding something.

- Show an interest in the people you meet. Ask about interesting aspects of their lives and/or work that you may have heard about.

- Follow your date's lead about how long your meeting should last. Be ready to leave when he or she is ready.

- Express your opinions respectfully if you disagree with something that is said.

> **Everyone's worst nightmare of meeting their date's parents was the topic of the 2000 film titled <u>Meet the Parents</u>, which starred Robert De Niro and Ben Stiller.**

- Understand the proper significance of meeting your date's parents. Is it just so they will know whom their child is with, or are you meeting them because they may become your in-laws?

- Pay attention to children and pets that may be present. They're part of the family package, too.

- Try to fit in with whatever plans have been made. If dinner is served, try to find something you like. Or if you see a movie, try to enjoy it.

- Think before you speak.

- Be sure any gifts you offer, such as a hostess gift for dinner, are appropriate. For example, do not bring alcohol if they do not drink.

"Ain't No Mountain High Enough": Meeting Your Date's Parents

- Respect their house rules if your meeting is in their home. If you are to be a house guest, respect their feelings about sleeping separately. It's their house.

- Accept food or drink if offered. If there is a legitimate reason you cannot, offer a brief explanation.

- Try to eat most, if not all, of your food if you eat dinner with them.

- Apologize immediately and sincerely if you offend them in any way.

- Thank his or her parents for any meal or entertainment that you may have had during the evening. At the very least, let them know you enjoyed meeting them.

> "To live without loving is to not really live."
>
> Molière

"Are You Lonesome Tonight": Dating as a Single Parent

"Are You Lonesome Tonight": Dating as a Single Parent

People become single parents through a variety of circumstances. Whether they are divorced or widowed, or maybe they have never married, their children add a mix to dating that few things can, and are an important consideration. Listed below are some things that should be considered if you have children and are dating.

What NOT to Do

- Do not rush into a relationship without realizing that not only is your wellbeing at risk, but your children's as well. They will be affected by a breakup if the relationship doesn't work out.

- Do not expect your children to feel as excited about your dates as you do. Expect a variety of emotions from them.

- Do not ask your date to your home before the relationship becomes serious. He or she should not get close to your children emotionally until you are both sure you have a future together.

- Do not introduce all of your dates to your children if you are dating more than one person.

- Do not ignore your child's opinion of your date once they are introduced.

- Do not allow your children to ruin your date so you will stay home with them.

> **The U.S. Census reports that 48 percent of all households are headed by unmarried individuals.**

- Do not date to simply find a new parent for your children.

"Are You Lonesome Tonight": Dating as a Single Parent

- Do not share inappropriate details about your dates with your children.

- Do not let your children see you in bed with anyone.

- Do not hide the fact that you are a parent from your date.

- Do not forego important occasions in your child's life to go on a date.

- Do not allow your date to treat your children with disrespect.

- Do not lie to your children if they ask you about your relationship. Offer answers appropriate for their age.

- Do not share details of a date with others if your children might overhear.

What to Do

- Date when you are ready, not when other people tell you that you should or shouldn't.

- Think seriously about whether the person you want to date might be a suitable parent for your children.

- Talk to your children.

- Be aware of expressing affection in front of your children.

- Make sure your children are cared for by someone responsible while you are out on a date. This will allow you to relax and enjoy yourself.

> In Shakespeare's time, people used to brush their teeth with sugar to preserve a sweet, kissable breath, which contributed to the poor oral hygiene of that era.

"Are You Lonesome Tonight": Dating as a Single Parent

- Be patient with yourself. It may take time to feel comfortable dating as a single parent, but do not expect too much of yourself too soon.

- Take it slowly.

- Introduce your date to your child as your friend until you are sure the relationship is serious.

- Find out how your date feels about children during one of your early meetings together.

- Make your children a higher priority than your date.

- Be particularly careful to treat your date with respect in front of your children. Use the opportunity to pattern behavior that your child will need to know when he or she is old enough to date.

> "For only as we ourselves, as adults, actually move and have our being in the state of love, can we be appropriate models and guides for our children. What we are teaches the child far more than what we say, so we must be what we want our children to become."
>
> Joseph Chilton Pearce

"To Know You Is to Love You": Office Romances

"To Know You Is to Love You": Office Romances

Before you decide to date a co-worker, give serious thought to how your job and your relationship might be affected. Here are some things to consider before you begin an office romance.

What NOT to Do

- Do not date a co-worker without checking company policy on this.

- Do not continue to ask a co-worker for a date if you are initially refused. Asking is not against the law, but harrassment is.

- Do not date a co-worker at all if company policy prohibits it.

- Do not think you can sneak around and date each other without anyone finding out. The truth always comes out, and usually at the worst time.

- Do not date anyone senior to you.

- Do not let your office romance interfere with your work.

> "Love does not consist of gazing at each other, but in looking together in the same direction."
> — Antoine de Saint-Exupery

- Do not share intimate details of your relationship with other co-workers.

- Do not bring disagreements into the office and let them affect your work or your co-workers.

- Do not ask co-workers to take sides if you and your co-worker/lover have a disagreement.

- Do not share details of any disagreement you might have.

"To Know You Is to Love You": Office Romances

- Do not send suggestive or explicit e-mails to your co-worker/lover, even if dating a co-worker is not prohibited by personnel guidelines.

- Do not call the object of your affection by pet names in the office.

- Do not make public displays of affection in the office.

What to Do

- Find out what office policy is about dating a co-worker and adhere to it.

- Make sure your interest is returned by the other party before pursuing a relationship; otherwise, he or she may report your overtures to administration.

- Let your boss know if you and a co-worker develop a personal relationship. Do not let him or her find out by accident.

- Take advantage of your time together in the office to learn about your co-worker in different situations.

- Be cautious about offering details of your relationship to other co-workers. Knowing too much of your relationship will make everyone uncomfortable.

> It is estimated that ten thousand marriages a year are the result of romances which began during coffee breaks.

- Be honest if asked if you have a relationship with a co-worker.

- Discuss at the beginning of your relationship how you will handle yourselves together in the office if you break up later.

"To Know You Is to Love You": Office Romances

- Realize that you may be the subject of office gossip if you date a co-worker.

- Focus on your business relationship, not your personal relationship when you are in meetings together, or when you go on business trips together.

- Set clear guidelines between the two of you on how you will behave in the office while dating.

- Be prepared to excuse yourself from situations that might present a conflict of interests because of your work/personal relationship.

- Find out what company policy says about married couples working together if it looks like you and your partner are moving toward a walk down the aisle.

- Have a plan for one of you to look for another job if you plan to marry and learn that you may not continue to work together.

"I Just Called to Say I Love You": Long Distance Relationships

"I Just Called to Say I Love You": Long Distance Relationships

So you've met someone in another city, or maybe your partner has moved away. Long distance relationships take patience, effort, and understanding. Here are some things to consider as you try to keep the relationship together.

What NOT to Do

- Do not assume that the relationship does not need maintenance.

- Do not assume that it will not last because of the separation.

- Do not jump to conclusions and assume the worst if something happens that you don't understand. Make time to talk about it and clear the air.

- Do not let misunderstandings fester. Deal with them as they happen.

- Do not dwell on small disappointments.

> "The pain of parting is nothing to the joy of meeting again."
> — Charles Dickens

- Do not habitually be out or unavailable when your partner tries to contact you.

- Do not fail to return calls from your partner.

- Do not interrogate your partner about his or her activities and friends.

- Do not continue with a long distance relationship just because you fear being alone.

- Do not lose focus of the big picture. Try to dismiss small inconveniences that are bound to occur.

"I Just Called to Say I Love You": Long Distance Relationships

What to Do

- Make the relationship a high priority.

- Keep in touch frequently by calling or sending cards and/or letters.

> "Distance is just a test to see how far love can travel."
>
> Anonymous

- Make sure you both clearly understand the terms of your relationship, whether it is exclusive, etc.

- Plan times to get together in person. Having a date to look forward to can help you get through the difficult times.

- Look for ways to reduce travel and phone call expenses.

- Reaffirm your feelings for your partner frequently.

- Share pictures that will help keep you abreast of daily activities.

- Surprise your loved one with an unexpected visit or reminders of your commitment.

- Keep your partner informed about your activities and interests.

> The first transatlantic wedding took place on December 2, 1933. The groom was in Michigan, the bride, in Sweden. The ceremony took 7 minutes and cost $47.50.

- Share expenses for travel, calls, and other communications.

- Talk openly together about how you feel about being apart. Be honest about your concerns for the effect on your relationship.

- Trust each other.

"I Just Called to Say I Love You": Long Distance Relationships

- Make an effort to know each other's friends, and to introduce yours to him or her.

- Express appreciation to your partner for his or her efforts to maintain your relationship.

- Focus on the future. Make plans to live in the same city as soon as possible.

> "Love is missing someone whenever you're apart, but somehow feeling warm inside because you're close in heart."
>
> Kay Knudsen

"You Don't Bring Me Flowers": Giving Gifts to Your Loved One

"You Don't Bring Me Flowers": Giving Gifts to Your Loved One

Giving gifts is one way to express your feelings. Here are some tried-and-true ways to help make sure your gifts are appropriate and thoughtful.

What NOT to Do

- Do not let important occasions go by without acknowledging them with a gift or at least a thoughtful card.

- Do not buy the same type of gifts for the same occasion every time.

- Do not recycle gifts. You are bound to be found out eventually.

- Do not give gifts out of obligation.

- Do not put more emphasis on how much is spent on a gift than the thought behind it.

- Do not buy expensive gifts too early in your relationship. A hefty price tag may imply that you think the relationship is further along than the other person thinks.

- Do not give gifts that the other person may already have. For example, if your partner is a florist, he or she would probably appreciate something other than flowers for a special occasion.

- Do not be late with your gift. A birthday present that is late will probably not be appreciated.

Food items are common gifts, especially those that are thought to be aphrodisiacs: almonds, asparagus, avocado, bananas, carrots, caviar, champagne, chocolate, figs, ginger, nutmeg, oysters, and truffles.

"You Don't Bring Me Flowers": Giving Gifts to Your Loved One

- Do not forget to wrap your gift nicely. A nice package can make even a modest gift special.

- Do not reveal disappointment if your partner gives you a gift that is not what you had hoped for. Try to appreciate the thought behind the effort.

> The largest box of chocolates on record was made on November 14, 2002, when Marshall Field's of Chicago made a box that weighed 3,226 pounds, and contained 90,090 individual chocolates.

What to Do

- Buy gifts with your partner in mind, not yourself.

- Hand-write a note or poem to accompany your gift.

- Consider what hobbies and special interests you can honor when buying a gift for your partner.

- Take into account cultural and religious preferences of the intended recipient when buying a gift for your loved one.

> Bored with traditional lovers' gifts? Consider giving something unusual, like kissing fish, to let your loved one know what's on your mind!

- Consider giving an intangible gift, such as a mystery date. Make sure the destination is somewhere your loved one will enjoy, and do not divulge details until the proper time.

"You Don't Bring Me Flowers": Giving Gifts to Your Loved One

- When sending flowers, check to see what each type symbolizes. Here are some flowers that are often sent, and the thoughts and emotions that they signify.

Flower	Meaning
Anemone	Love is dying
Carnation	Joy
Chrysanthemum	Hope
Daffodil	Desire
Daisy	Innocence
Forget-me-not	True love and constancy
Gladioli	Strength
Lily	Devotion
Pansy	Loving thoughts
Poppy	Consolation
Red rose	Passion
Sunflower	Warm feelings
Sweet Pea	Gratitude
Tulip	Luck
Violet	Modesty
White rosebud	Purity
Yellow rose	Jealousy

- Roses, in particular, have romantic connotations. Even different colors of roses have different meanings. Here are some particular roses and what they mean:

Color	Meaning
Lavender	Love at first sight
Moss rose	I admire you from afar.

"You Don't Bring Me Flowers": Giving Gifts to Your Loved One

Orange/coral	Desire
Pale of any color	Friendship
Pink	Appreciation or gratitude
Purple	I will love you forever.
Red	True love
White	I love you not.
Wild rose	Uncontrollable desire
Yellow	Jealousy

- Think of new and different ways to present your gift.
- Be as diplomatic as possible if a gift you receive absolutely must be exchanged.

> Roses are estimated to account for 40 percent of all the gifts given on Valentine's Day.

"Have I Told You Lately that I Love You?": Writing a Love Letter

"Have I Told You Lately that I Love You?": Writing a Love Letter

There are few things more sentimental than a love letter. It expresses thoughts that may be difficult to express verbally, and is also a wonderful keepsake that can be re-read. Make yours special by following the suggestions below.

What NOT to Do

- Do not write anything that will make the other person feel uncomfortable.

- Do not be overly romantic if you know your partner is not the "mushy" type.

> "At the touch of love, everyone becomes a poet."
> Plato

- Do not let anyone else read the letter you will send to your partner. The letter is personal and should be kept between the two of you.

- Do not type your letter. It should be in your own best handwriting.

- Do not use big words or stilted language. Be conversational.

- Do not write about anyone but you and your lover.

- Do not feel that the letter must be long. A simple heartfelt expression is more treasured than longer letters with no real meaning.

- Do not send your letter with crossed-out words or corrections in the writing. Re-write the letter until it is perfect.

- Do not send letters on smudged or creased paper.

- Do not be disappointed if you don't get a love letter in return. You are writing to express your feelings, not to elicit a response.

"Have I Told You Lately that I Love You?": Writing a Love Letter

> Lovers who send their sentiments in Valentine cards can thank Esther Howland, Mother of the American Valentine. Howland, a contemporary of Emily Dickinson, received a Valentine card from an acquaintance in England, and decided she could mass-produce them in her own country. She made a dozen lace and paper samples, hoping for as much as $200 in orders. She was stunned at the $5,000 in advance sales they created. She recruited friends and family for an assembly line to fill the orders, and a new business was born.

What to Do

- Decide why you are writing. Is it to say you miss your partner in an established relationship, or is it to declare feelings for the first time?

- Select paper that will complement your words. Choose an elegant note card or stationery if you intend to write something formal, or a torn-out sheet from a notebook if you intend to be casual and light-hearted.

- Consider other creative ways to express yourself, such as writing your thoughts on a mirror, or on a menu of a restaurant where you intend to go together.

- Date your letter so you'll have a record of when it was sent. You may want to reminisce later.

- Describe how your loved one makes you feel.

- Be sincere. Do not use clichés.

"Have I Told You Lately that I Love You?": Writing a Love Letter

- Recall a wonderful time together and what it meant to you.
- Use your best penmanship.
- Write your letter with dark ink.
- Try to be original, but above all, be sincere.
- Add artwork if you have the talent for it.
- Use proper grammar and spelling.
- Write a draft, set it aside for a while, then read it again.
- Mention specific things that you find attractive about your loved one.
- Recall your times together, or, if writing to someone new, your hopes for the future.
- Close with an expression of hoping to see the other person soon.
- Include an appropriate closing, such as "Love," or "Always yours."
- Read your letter several times to make sure it says what you intended.
- Consider adding a flower or poem, or other unusual item to the note.

> The tradition of using an X to represent a kiss started in medieval times, when those who could not write signed documents with an X, then placed a kiss upon the X to show sincerity. The kiss became synonymous with the X, which came to be commonly used at the end of letters as kiss symbols.

"Have I Told You Lately that I Love You?": Writing a Love Letter

> Letters from their sweeties aren't the only place where people like to read about love. Romance novels comprise 53 percent of all mass market paperback sales in the U.S.

- Deliver your letter in an unusual way, or leave it in a place special to your relationship.

- Surprise your partner by leaving a note in an unexpected place, such as slipping a note into luggage when he or she is going away. The letter will be a nice surprise when he or she starts to unpack.

- Make sure the letter doesn't get into the wrong hands. It is personal between you and your loved one.

"I'm Sorry": Resolving Conflict

"I'm Sorry": Resolving Conflict

Even in the best of relationships, conflict is bound to arise occasionally. Use the items below to help deal with differences as they arise, before they become larger.

What NOT to Do

- Do not avoid conflict. If there is a difference of opinion, it needs to be expressed.

- Do not ignore signs that there is a problem in your relationship.

- Do not hesitate to address the problem. Waiting will only allow it to fester.

- Do not remind your partner of past offenses.

- Do not bring up old issues in current disagreements.

- Do not insist on talking when the other person has indicated that he or she is not ready.

- Do not raise your voice to each other.

- Do not use accusatory words, like "You always..." and "You never...." Instead, be specific about the issue at hand.

- Do not threaten to terminate the relationship every time there is conflict.

- Do not blurt out your thoughts without thinking about them. Consider the best way to express your feelings.

> "Love looks not with the eyes, but with the mind; And therefore is winged Cupid painted blind."
>
> William Shakespeare,
> *A Midsummer Night's Dream*

"I'm Sorry": Resolving Conflict

- Do not talk about your disagreements to other people, particularly in public.

- Do not be defensive if your partner brings up something that has offended him or her.

- Do not try to intimidate the other person into agreeing with you. Nothing will be solved until you both express your honest opinions.

- Do not make negative personal remarks about each other, or call each other names.

- Do not pretend to agree with your partner for the sake of peace. You should be able to express your true feelings in a close relationship.

- Do not interrupt the other person when he or she is expressing an opinion.

- Do not hang up on a phone conversation or walk away while your partner is trying to express his or her opinion.

- Do not use personal information that you know about your partner against him or her in times of disagreement.

- Do not try to settle disagreements in the heat of the moment. Wait until you have both calmed down to discuss things rationally.

- Do not drag third parties into the fray, like your mother or mother-in-law.

What to Do
- Make sure your attitude reflects a desire to resolve conflict. If all you want to do is prove how right you are, nothing will be accomplished.

"I'm Sorry": Resolving Conflict

- Deal with even small issues before they have a chance to fester.
- Discuss things from a "we" perspective. The problem is "ours," not "yours."
- Try to see the other person's point of view.
- Try to settle things at a time when there are no distractions.
- Agree to hear each other out completely when there is a difference of opinion.
- Stay calm and be direct.
- Focus on the big picture. Is the issue so big that you are willing to jeopardize your relationship over it?
- Communicate your honest feelings. This is not a game.
- Agree to compromise on decisions if you are unable to settle on solutions that either of you want.
- Own your part in the problem.
- Look for patterns and recurring issues in your conflicts and try to get to the real root of the problem.
- Discuss what steps are necessary to prevent the same problem from happening again.
- Keep your disagreements between the two of you. Other people do not need to know your business.
- Let go of issues once they've been dealt with.

> "Love is what you've been through with somebody."
> — James Thurber

"Your Cheatin' Heart": Handling an Unfaithful Lover

"Your Cheatin' Heart": Handling an Unfaithful Lover

The hurt and disappointment of learning that your lover has been unfaithful is difficult to manage, but you can get through it. Here are some suggestions that may help.

What NOT to Do

- Do not blame yourself for the other person's actions.

- Do not allow yourself to be manipulated with promises that the other person will never cheat again.

- Do not remain in a relationship where you are not treated respectfully.

- Do not resort to childish acts of retaliation.

- Do not share sordid details about the situation with others.

> **Fifteen percent of married women and 22 percent of married men have engaged in extramarital affairs.**

- Do not make a spur-of-the-moment decision that you might regret. Give yourself time to think rationally about the best course of action.

- Do not allow other people to interfere in the situation. The problem is between the two of you.

What to Do

- Accept and acknowledge your feelings of anger and betrayal.

- Set aside your emotions and try to look at the situation objectively. What advice would you give a friend in your situation?

"Your Cheatin' Heart": Handling an Unfaithful Lover

- Confront your partner and let him or her know exactly how you feel.
- Try to find out why the unfaithfulness occurred.
- Listen if the other person tries to explain his or her behavior.
- Evaluate whether your partner's behavior has permanently destroyed your trust, and if the relationship can be salvaged.
- Find a constructive outlet for your emotions.
- Allow yourself time to get over the disappointment of the betrayal.

Reflecting a sign of the times, there is finally a greeting card for adulterers. The response to the Secret Lover Collection has been "phenomenal," according to creator Cathy Gallagher. Twenty-four cards offer a variety of messages "to capture and express the unique emotional bond and intensity between lovers involved in this type of relationship."

"Bye Bye Love": Breaking Up

"Bye Bye Love": Breaking Up

Leaving a relationship for any reason is hard, but sometimes it is necessary. Make the best of a bad situation by following these pointers.

What NOT to Do

- Do not delay the inevitable. If you think the relationship is over, break it off.

- Do not stay in an unsatisfying relationship just because you are afraid to be alone. There are worse things.

- Do not stay in a bad or abusive relationship for children. Most experts agree that this does more harm than good.

- Do not delay a break up because you fear what people will say or think.

- Do not expect yourself to get over the loss quickly.

> "Better to have loved and lost, than to have never loved at all."
> Saint Augustine

- Do not tell anyone else before you tell the person you are breaking up with. He or she should hear from you, and not from a third party that might rush in with the news.

- Do not do anything following your loss that you will regret later. Moving to a new apartment may offer new scenery, but your loss will still be with you.

- Do not dwell on details of the relationship that are upsetting. Avoid "your" favorite songs and places, at least for a while.

- Do not break up with the person on a day that has special significance to him or her, such as a birthday.

"Bye Bye Love": Breaking Up

- Do not continue to pry into details of your ex's life, hoping to confirm or disprove facts that may have led to the breakup. You will probably find out something you would be better off not knowing.

- Do not continue to call your former partner after the breakup. It will not accomplish anything, and you will appear to be desperate.

- Do not blame the other person for your part in the breakup.

- Do not hang on to mementos or personal items that may be upsetting. Even if you do not want to discard them, at least put them away until you heal from the loss.

- Do not break up on the phone, in a letter, or by e-mail.

- Do not backtrack.

- Do not allow the other person to manipulate you into staying in the relationship if you truly want out.

> "The hottest love has the coldest end."
> Socrates

- Do not try to remain friends unless both people are honestly willing to accept responsibility for what went wrong.

- Do not reveal personal details about the other person that you learned during the relationship.

- Do not say untrue things about the other person to make yourself look better.

- Do not rush into another relationship until you have had time to heal from the one you've just lost.

- Do not carry expectations into your next relationship based on deficiencies in this one.

"Bye Bye Love": Breaking Up

- Do not let this experience keep you from being open to another relationship later.

What to Do

- Be realistic. If you suspect that the relationship might have run its course, admit it. If you are being abused or cheated on, your decision should be obvious.

- Get out immediately if the relationship becomes abusive. Make your safety a priority.

- Make a clean break. Don't try to invent reasons to contact him or her.

- Think about your future. If your partner is jealous or possessive, will you be able to live with that on a long-term basis?

- Evaluate your role in the relationship. If you are doing all the work, it is time to admit that it might be over.

- Pick a time for the breakup. Be careful not to choose times that might already be difficult for the other person, for instance, if there has been a death in the family.

- Accept responsibility for your part in the breakup of the relationship.

- Choose a private place for your conversation.

- Allow yourself time to grieve the loss.

- Make deliberate efforts to build up your confidence and independence.

- Ask for your personal items that the other person might have.

"Bye Bye Love": Breaking Up

- Erase your ex's phone number and e-mail address from your phone and computer.

- Take up a new hobby or enroll in a class that interests you. Not only will it help distract you from your loss, but it will help you develop something new and interesting about yourself or meet new people.

- Indulge and pamper yourself following the loss. Be your own best friend and do things you like to do.

- Give yourself permission to feel bad about the loss.

> "Nothing takes the taste out of peanut butter quite like unrequited love."
> — Charlie Brown

- Get plenty of rest, eat properly, and exercise. Your loss is an emotional one, but can have physical side effects if you do not take care of yourself.

- See your doctor if you have trouble sleeping, or are unable to get over the sadness after an appropriate amount of time.

- Join a support group to help you through the loss.

- Talk to your friends about the loss.

- Get a journal and write down your thoughts and feelings as you grieve.

- Learn to go out again, even if you must go out alone.

- Date other people when you have the opportunity. Every date doesn't have to result in a long-term relationship, and you may meet someone you are really interested in getting to know.

"Bye Bye Love": Breaking Up

- Examine what went wrong in the relationship so you can avoid making the same mistakes again.
- Look for patterns in your relationships and work to correct actions that commonly cause problems.
- Stay away from one-on-one situations for a while.
- Forgive your former partner for hurts done to you, and move on.

> "Love is never lost. If not reciprocated, it will flow back and soften and purify the heart."
> Washington Irving

"With This Ring": Buying an Engagement Ring

"With This Ring": Buying an Engagement Ring

Buying a ring is an emotional yet expensive experience. Minimize the stress by following the suggestions listed below.

What NOT to Do

- Do not spend everything you have on an engagement ring. With a wedding to plan, and a household to establish, you will have other expenses to consider in addition to the ring.

- Do not make a hasty decision about a ring.

- Do not give a ring that was bought for someone else.

- Do not buy from a jeweler without knowing his credentials.

> The engagement ring is a popular symbol of betrothal in western society. It began in 1477 when Archduke Maximillian of Austria presented Mary of Burgundy a diamond ring to seal their engagement. A diamond was chosen because it was considered to be a talisman of good fortune for a couple.

- Do not have a ring engraved without knowing it fits. The engraving may be damaged if you have to adjust the size.

- Do not show others the ring before you give it to your intended. Let him or her be the one to "show it off" once you've popped the question.

"With This Ring": Buying an Engagement Ring

What to Do

- Decide what style of ring you want. Particulars to consider are type of metal, type of stone, shape of the stone, and, of course, the cost.

- Know ahead of time whether he or she would like to be surprised with a ring, or would like to help with the selection.

> Traditionally, the industry standard for how much one should spend on a diamond has been two months' salary. Some experts suggest no more than six weeks' salary, or 6 percent of a year's income.

- In case your intended would like to be surprised, here are some ways to get the information you need:

    - Ask his or her best friend.
    - Take one of his or her rings to the jeweler to determine the size you should buy.
    - Examine his or her current jewelry for metal and style preferences.
    - Keep mental notes of his or her comments about rings when the subject comes up in casual conversation.
    - Ask the jeweler if you will be able to exchange the ring if your selection is not satisfactory.

- Familiarize yourself with the four Cs if you intend to choose a diamond ring: Carat, Clarity, Color, and Cut.

    Carat – a diamond's weight. A diamond's size is measured in carat weight, and each carat is equal to 100 points. Large diamonds are rarer than small ones, and a bigger diamond

"With This Ring": Buying an Engagement Ring

may show off its features to better advantage. But there are other factors to consider, since even diamonds of identical size may vary in value because of other important characteristics.

Clarity – the purity of a diamond. Virtually all diamonds contain unique characteristics that are invisible to the naked eye, but can be seen with a jeweler's magnifying loupe. These natural markings, called inclusions, may appear as tiny lusters or clouds. The number, color, type, size, and position of these affect a diamond's clarity. The greater a stone's clarity, the more brilliant, and therefore, the more valuable it is. Here are some abbreviations used by jewelers to express clarity:
- FL (flawless)
- IF (internally flawless)
- WS1 WS2 (very small inclusions)
- SI1 SI2 SI3 (small inclusions)
- I1 I2 I3 (visible inclusions)

Color – a diamond's whiteness. The ideal diamond is colorless. The closer a diamond is to being colorless, the more vividly it can reflect light and colors of the spectrum. While most diamonds appear to be colorless, close observation may reveal subtle yellow or brown tones. Here are some abbreviations used to distinguish color:
- D E F (colorless)
- G H I J (near colorless)
- K L M (faint yellow)
- N O P Q R (very light yellow)
- S T U V W X Y Z (light yellow)

"With This Ring": Buying an Engagement Ring

There are, however, "fancy" diamonds in well-defined colors such as red, pink, blue, green, and canary yellow that are highly prized and are as rare as colorless stones.

Cut – a diamond's brilliance. A proper cut can release the sparkle and beauty in a diamond. A master cutter can cut a stone so that light bounces from one facet to another and disperses through the top of the stone. An improperly cut stone will be less brilliant than a properly cut one. The types of cut include round, oval, marquise, square (princess), rectangular (emerald), pear, heart, and trillion (triangle).

- Consider buying wedding bands at the same time as the engagement ring since they often come in sets. Also, you may get a better price.

- Visit several jewelers to allow yourself a wide variety of rings from which to choose.

- Keep your receipt.

- Insure the ring.

- Get an appraisal of the value of the ring in writing.

- Store documents about the ring in a secure place.

- Have your jeweler inspect the ring once a year for loose stones.

> **About 75 percent of first-time brides will receive a diamond engagement ring (67 percent of repeat brides). A third of men's wedding rings have diamonds.**

"Hopelessly Devoted to You": Proposing

"Hopelessly Devoted to You": Proposing

If you're thinking of proposing, you want to be sure to do it right! Here are some suggestions to make this special time go without a hitch.

What NOT to Do

- Do not propose until you are absolutely sure you are ready. Do not be pressured into it by anyone or anything.

- Do not propose if your intended has been evasive about a commitment or reluctant to discuss marriage.

- Do not spend too much on setting up the proposal. Be careful not to let the expense of staging it upstage the actual event.

- Do not make overly elaborate plans to orchestrate the proposal. Sometimes the more plans you make, the more things there are to go wrong.

St. Valentine was a priest in Rome, and was condemned to death on February 14, AD 269, for helping Christian martyrs. He had also secretly married men in the army, though Claudius II had prohibited marriage for military men, thinking it would sap their strength. As he awaited his execution in prison, St. Valentine fell in love with the jailor's blind daughter. It is said that his love for her, and his faith, healed her from her blindness before his death. Upon his death, he left a note for her signed "From Your Valentine," a phrase used since that time by lovers to express affection.

"Hopelessly Devoted to You": Proposing

- Do not give an ultimatum to get someone to marry you. You want them to marry you out of love, not out of fear of losing you.

- Do not propose in an effort to secure a shaky relationship.

- Do not propose just to give your children another parent.

- Do not be hard on yourself if your proposal plans go awry. Try to laugh about it and use it as a funny story about your new life together.

What to Do

- Talk with your partner's parents to get their blessing if that will be important to him or her.

- Decide if you will propose with or without a ring, and plan accordingly.

- Anticipate the response of your lover, and be prepared for all possible scenarios.

- Set the stage. Pick a spot that is special to you, or that has particular significance to your relationship.

- Choose the proper time to propose. Do not pop the question if he or she is under unusual stress, or do it on a day that has a negative connotation, such as April Fool's Day.

> "By all means marry. If you get a good wife, you'll be happy. If you get a bad one, you'll become a philosopher...and that is a good thing for any man."
>
> Socrates

"Hopelessly Devoted to You": Proposing

- Be prepared in case your intended asks for time to think.

- If you plan the proposal to be a surprise, do not tell anyone at all, unless you need to talk with your loved ones' parents first. The more people that know, the more likely the news will get to your partner prematurely.

- Try not to spoil your own surprise by being unusually nervous or concerned about details.

- Share news of your engagement with your children, if there are any, and then with your parents. Typically, the bride-to-be's parents are told first.

> **Six percent of men propose to their girlfriends over the phone.**

"Get Me to the Church on Time": Planning a Wedding

"Get Me to the Church on Time": Planning a Wedding

Weddings are one of the biggest events in a person's/couple's life, so every effort should be made to make it a success. That are many factors involved in making a wedding a success, and careful attention should be paid to all of them, big and small.

What NOT to Do

- Do not include children if you do not want to. Make sure to address the invitation to only those who are actually invited. It is not proper to put "No children" or "Adults only."

- Do not try to please others by doing your wedding like they want it. It's your wedding. Do it your way.

- Do not register for gifts at too many places.

- Do not register for gifts that you do not need, thinking you will return them for cash.

- Do not make major decisions without consulting your fiancé(e).

- Do not discuss the cost of any aspect of the wedding with others.

- Do not choose elaborate and expensive outfits and accessories for your attendants.

Save-the-date cards may be sent about six months before the wedding to give people advance notice to reserve your wedding date on their calendar. These are particularly helpful if you will be married during the holidays, or at other times when calendars might be crowded by the time formal invitations arrive.

"Get Me to the Church on Time": Planning a Wedding

- Do not try to invite everyone you know to your wedding.
- Do not recall invitations unless the wedding has been cancelled.
- Do not keep wedding gifts if the wedding is called off for any reason.

What to Do
- Start your planning early.
- Leave enough time to handle all the details.
- Devise a budget and stick to it as much as possible.
- Remember that the marriage is the most important thing, not the wedding.
- Take advantage of a professional wedding planner if possible. It will take some of the burden off your shoulders, and will leave you time to deal with other details that only you can handle.

> **Wedding veils came into vogue in the United States when Nelly Curtis wore a veil at her wedding to George Washington's aid, Major Lawrence Lewis. Major Lewis saw his bride-to-be standing behind a filmy curtain and commented to her how beautiful she appeared. She then decided to veil herself for their ceremony.**

- Ask professionals who will be helping you how much time they will need to get everything done properly.

"Get Me to the Church on Time": Planning a Wedding

- Select a date for your wedding that is not already notable for something else. Obvious dates to avoid would be Friday the 13th, April 1, September 11, and Daylight Savings Time transition days, which might be confusing to guests.

- Decide early on who will pay for what. Each couple must decide what works for them, but here are some traditional guidelines:

Bride's Family
- Bridal brunch
- Bridesmaids' luncheon
- Church fees
- Decorative items for the church and reception
- Flowers for church, bridesmaids, and reception
- Gifts for bridal party
- Groom's gift
- Groom's ring
- Janitorial workers
- Lodging for bridesmaids, if necessary
- Lodging for out-of-town guests
- Musician fees for the ceremony and reception
- Printed items such as invitations, programs, napkins, and wedding novelties
- Reception costs, including food venue, and entertainment
- Rice bags
- Wedding breakfast
- Wedding cake
- Wedding gown, headpiece, and accessories
- Wedding photos and videos

"Get Me to the Church on Time": Planning a Wedding

Groom's family
- Bride's bouquet
- Bride's gift
- Bride's ring
- Boutonnieres for groomsmen and ushers
- Clergy fees
- Corsages for mothers
- Gifts for groomsmen
- Groom's cake
- Honeymoon arrangements
- Limousine service for the bride and groom
- Lodging for groomsmen, if necessary
- Marriage license
- Rehearsal dinner

Bridal party
- Bridesmaid dress
- Gift for the couple
- The shower
- Transportation

Groomsmen
- Bachelor party
- Gift for the couple
- Tuxedo or suit
- Transportation

> "Henceforth there shall be such a oneness between us, that when one weeps, the other will taste salt."
>
> Unknown

- Choose attendants and other members of the wedding party with care. Not only will they be a part of your memories of your special day, but they will be a part of the photos that you will cherish.

"Get Me to the Church on Time": Planning a Wedding

- Try to choose outfits that your attendants really can wear later.

- Get details about goods and services in writing. There is nothing worse than thinking you are getting a particular product or service, and then finding out that you aren't.

- Find out deadlines by which you will have to have particular decisions made, and abide by them.

- Choose your invitations carefully. They should be an appropriate indication of the type of wedding you are planning.

- Order extra invitations and envelopes in case you make errors in addressing them.

- Make sure to spell guests's names correctly on invitations.

> **Eighty-five percent of weddings are held in a church or synagogue.**

- Include directions to the wedding, or a map if the location will be hard to find, or if there will be out-of-town guests.

- Check the amount of postage needed for each invitation, and affix the proper amount.

- Mail out invitations six to eight weeks before your wedding.

- Ask that your invitations be hand canceled at the post office.

- Check to see what religious restrictions you should observe, such as certain forms of clothing, or certain types of music that are not allowed.

- Consider providing a nursery area for children during the ceremony so that an infant's cry or a toddler's talk does not interrupt the service.

"Get Me to the Church on Time": Planning a Wedding

- Have a back-up plan if your wedding will be outdoors.

- Be ready to bear the expense of extras that you ask of your attendants, such as professionally applied make-up or perfect manicures.

- Check well ahead of the wedding for marriage license requirements.

- Show your appreciation to members of the wedding party with a gift to help commemorate the occasion.

- Send thank-you notes promptly so you do not feel overwhelmed by the task.

> **The groom is supposed to wear a flower that appears in the bridal bouquet in his buttonhole. This stems from the medieval tradition of a knight wearing his lady's colors as a declaration of his love.**

- Make sure the appropriate people have been invited to the rehearsal dinner.

- Remember to provide honorariums or payment to the minister, organist, and others who help with the ceremony but who are not attendants.

- Give careful thought to seat assignment for the reception. Do not seat guests together who do not get along, seat older guests away from loud music, etc.

- Consider special needs that guests may have when planning what foods to serve.

- Take time to enjoy your day!

"Get Me to the Church on Time": Planning a Wedding

The wedding cake has always been an important wedding tradition. In medieval times, guests brought small cakes, piled them on a table, and the new couple tried to kiss over them. An enterprising young baker decided to put all the cakes together, covered them with frosting, and the tiered wedding cake was born.

"There's a Place for Us": Arranging Your Honeymoon

"There's a Place for Us": Arranging Your Honeymoon

Going on a honeymoon gives you and your new spouse a chance to rest and relax after all the activity surrounding your wedding. It also offers you a chance to settle into your role as a married couple away from family and friends. Make your honeymoon one to remember by following the suggestions below.

What NOT to Do

- Do not expect that a wonderful honeymoon will just happen without planning. It won't.

- Do not wait until the last minute to make your plans.

- Do not be pressured into a trip that you know you do not want, even if it's a good deal.

- Do not be reluctant to ask questions about details of travel or accommodations. You need to know specifics to plan the trip you want.

> A recent survey of newlyweds found sun and surf to be popular ingredients for a romantic honeymoon. The top choice of location was Hawaii, followed by other sandy backdrops like Mexico, Jamaica, Tahiti, and Bermuda.

- Do not go into debt for an elaborate honeymoon that you cannot afford.

- Do not expect perfection. Relax and do not lose focus on the big picture.

"There's a Place for Us": Arranging Your Honeymoon

What to Do

- Decide with your fiancé(e) what type of trip you want and can afford.

- Consult a travel agent if you need help researching your options or making arrangements.

- Begin making your plans as soon as your wedding date has been set.

- Plan early and take advantage of special offers and discounts.

- Let people where you are staying know you are making honeymoon reservations. They may offer a special rate or room, and may even throw in some extras.

- Discuss your plans frequently with your fiancé(e) so that you do not duplicate your efforts.

- Allow sufficient money in your honeymoon budget to tip those who serve you.

Although June is typically regarded as the month for weddings, more weddings have been in August in the past decade than in June.

- Start a honeymoon registry. If you already have all the household items you need, you can customize your honeymoon expenses into gift-sized portions and receive gifts to cover those items.

- Include luggage and travel items in your registry as well.

"There's a Place for Us": Arranging Your Honeymoon

- If your destination is outside of the country, be sure to get your passports and visas in order well in advance.

- Allow for extended wait times due to security measures when planning your travel itinerary.

- Research weather conditions at your destination for the time you will be there, and plan appropriately.

- Exchange currency if your destination uses another monetary system.

- Make a list of things you will need to pack. You will have too many details to handle at the last minute to rely only on your memory for everything.

- Verify what kind of identification you will need for your travel. Make sure your name is correct on everything.

- Confirm all reservations the week of the wedding.

- Take care of logistics at home such as pets and mail by arranging for a friend to check them while you are away.

- Leave information with a trusted friend about how and where you can be contacted in case of an emergency.

"Love and Marriage": Enjoying Life as Newlyweds

"Love and Marriage": Enjoying Life as Newlyweds

The excitement of the courtship and wedding is over, and now you are settling into the special time of being a newlywed. Enjoy your new life together by following the tips below just for you.

What NOT to Do

- Do not pattern your marriage after anyone else's. Yours is unique and should be what you want it to be.

- Do not go into debt for luxury items.

- Do not exclude your friends from your life just because you're married now.

> "Take each other for better or worse but not for granted."
> — Arlene Dahl

- Do not just "let yourself go" because you no longer have to worry about getting a date.

- Do not talk unkindly about your spouse's family.

- Do not "hit below the belt" during disagreements.

The Newlywed Game originally aired from July 11, 1966, to December 20, 1974, for 2,195 episodes, and in syndication until 1980. Husbands and wives were separated in the studio and asked questions about how the other partner would respond. They earned points for correctly predicting their spouse's answer, and the couple with the most points at the end of the game won the grand prize.

"Love and Marriage": Enjoying Life as Newlyweds

- Do not expect your spouse to read your mind.

- Do not let misunderstandings drag on without trying to resolve them.

- Do not continue to cling to your family, and make your partner second place.

What to Do

- Talk openly about your expectations of marriage, and your new roles as husband and wife.

- Discuss the logistics of living together. For example, whose things go where in the bathroom?

- Share your expectations about who will do what jobs around the house.

Experts say the first year of marriage is the hardest. The film industry must think it's good box office material, too. Here are some movies that have dealt with the trials and the humor of that first year: The Cowboy and the Lady (1938), Apartment for Peggy (1948), I Was a Male War Bride (1949), The Quiet Man (1952), The Long, Long Trailer (1954), Barefoot in the Park (1967), Fools Rush In (1997), and Shrek 2 (2004).

- Continue to make time for each other.

- Decide before the wedding how money will be handled.

"Love and Marriage": Enjoying Life as Newlyweds

- Take care of debt associated with the wedding as soon as possible.

- Be honest with each other about the debts you already owe.

- Set up a financial plan for your future.

- Work to establish good relationships with both sets of parents, but establish boundaries for your new family.

- Decide as fairly as possible how you will spend holidays and with whose family.

- Allow a time for cooling off after arguments.

- Respect your partner's need for privacy in some areas. Do not read his or her e-mail or regular mail without permission.

- Pick your battles. Small things are not worth making issues of, and taking sides on them will do more harm than good.

- Learn to forgive each other for small hurts that are bound to occur in day-to-day living.

- Be loyal to your spouse. Do not talk unkindly about him or her to other people.

- Enjoy each stage of your life together. For example, don't be so obsessed with the larger home you will later own that you fail to appreciate the coziness of your starter home.

"Forever and Ever, Amen": Having a Happy Marriage

"Forever and Ever, Amen": Having a Happy Marriage

Every marriage is a unique agreement between two individuals with specific expectations, so there are no one-size-fits-all rules that apply. But the general suggestions below may be of help as you look forward to a long relationship together.

What NOT to Do

- Do not expect your marriage to be perfect. It won't be because it is not made up of perfect people.

- Do not forget to do the small things that were important when you dated.

- Do not let day-to-day life crowd out your time together.

- Do not betray your spouses' confidences to others.

> "It is not the lack of love, but a lack of friendship that makes unhappy marriages."
> — Friedrich Nietzsche

- Do not fantasize about who else you could be married to. The grass always seems greener elsewhere, but put your effort into the relationship at hand.

- Do not listen to other people's opinion about what your marriage should be like. You and your spouse should design it according to what you want.

A long-term study of middle-aged women has determined that wives in highly satisfying marriages have fewer risk factors for cardiovascular disease than their less-satisfied or unmarried counterparts.

"Forever and Ever, Amen": Having a Happy Marriage

- Do not take your marriage for granted.

- Do not be angry at the same time.

- Do not say everything that comes to mind during a disagreement. Think of the best way to express your thoughts so that you do not have to do damage repair later.

- Do not favor your own family over your partner's. Treat both sides equally.

What to Do
- Be committed to the relationship. Think in terms of "we" instead of "me."

- Make your spouse's needs a priority.

> "Marriage is a great institution, but I'm not ready for an institution."
> Mae West

- Make time to communicate about everything, even things you might not agree on. Communication is essential to a good relationship.

- Offer constructive comments, not criticism, when needed.

- Celebrate special dates, such as the anniversary of the day you met.

- Resolve conflict as it occurs.

- Be as courteous to your spouse in everyday situations as you are on special occasions.

- Be willing to admit when you are wrong.

- Set aside time to spend together, even after children come, and when schedules are busy.

"Forever and Ever, Amen": Having a Happy Marriage

> **Planning to renew your vows? The bride may still wear white as a sign of joy, but trains are usually worn by those who have never been married. And if you discourage gifts, don't mention it on the invitation; pass that information by word of mouth.**

- Keep problems and disagreements between the two of you.
- Get outside help when problems are bigger than the two of you can handle.
- Find hobbies and activities that you can enjoy together.
- Express affection often.
- Let your partner know frequently how much you appreciate the things he or she does for you.
- Listen to your partner's opinion about big and small issues. You don't have to agree with it, but you do need to respect it.
- Live within your means. Overspending can lead to major marital problems.

If You Liked *What NOT to Do in Love!*, You'll Enjoy Other Books in This Series

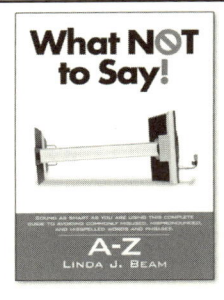

ISBN: 1-58173-360-7
$7.95
What NOT to Say! is an indispensable guide to words and phrases that are often mispronounced, misspelled, and misused.

ISBN: 1-58173-318-6
$7.95
What NOT to Name Your Baby! can help you choose a name for your child that will be a blessing instead of a burden.

ISBN: 1-58173-405-0
$7.95
What NOT to Do in Polite Company! addresses personal and professional etiquette issues specific to our culture.

ISBN: 1-58173-408-5
$7.95
What NOT to Do at Work! will help you treat your co-workers, boss, and clients with the respect and courtesy they want and deserve.